D0601596

super simple ice projects

FUN AND EASY CRAFTS INSPIRED BY NATURE

Kelly Doudna

Consulting Editor, Diane Craig, M.A./Reading Specialist

A Division of ABDO

ABDO
Publishing Company

visit us at www.abdopublishing.com

Published by ABDO Publishing Company, a division of ABDO, P.O. Box 398166, Minneapolis, Minnesota 55439.
Copyright © 2014 by Abdo Consulting Group, Inc. International copyrights reserved in all countries. No part of this book may be reproduced in any form without written permission from the publisher. Super SandCastle™ is a trademark and logo of ABDO Publishing Company.

Printed in the United States of America, North Mankato, Minnesota
102013
012014

♻ PRINTED ON RECYCLED PAPER

Editor: Liz Salzmann
Content Developer: Nancy Tuminelly
Cover and Interior Design and Production: Kelly Doudna, Mighty Media, Inc.
Photo Credits: Kelly Doudna, Shutterstock

The following manufacturer's name appearing in this book is a trademark: Dixie®

Library of Congress Cataloging-in-Publication Data
Doudna, Kelly, 1963-
  Super simple ice projects : fun and easy crafts inspired by nature / Kelly Doudna ; consulting editor, Diane Craig, M.A./reading specialist.
    pages cm. -- (Super simple nature crafts)
  Audience: Age 5-10.
  ISBN 978-1-62403-078-9
1. Handicraft--Juvenile literature. 2. Nature craft--Juvenile literature. 3. Ice--Juvenile literature. I. Title.
TT145.D68 2014
  745.59--dc23
                    2013022900

Super SandCastle™ books are created by a team of professional educators, reading specialists, and content developers around five essential components—phonemic awareness, phonics, vocabulary, text comprehension, and fluency—to assist young readers as they develop reading skills and strategies and increase their general knowledge. All books are written, reviewed, and leveled for guided reading, early reading intervention, and Accelerated Reader® programs for use in shared, guided, and independent reading and writing activities to support a balanced approach to literacy instruction.

TO ADULT HELPERS

The craft projects in this series are fun and simple. There are just a few things to remember to keep kids safe. Some projects require the use of sharp or hot objects. Also, kids may be using messy materials such as glue or paint. Make sure they protect their clothes and work surfaces. Review the projects before starting, and be ready to assist when necessary.

KEY SYMBOL

Look for this warning symbol in this book.

SHARP!
You will be working with a sharp object. Get help!

contents

interesting ice

We love ice cubes in a cold drink on a hot day. We hope we don't slip on an icy patch in the winter. But did you know you can get crafty with ice? Use the cold air of winter outside or your freezer inside. Think outside the ice cube tray!

Try the fun and simple projects in this book. You'll find out how interesting ice can be!

Ice cubes, **icicles**, and frozen lakes all happen when water freezes and becomes ice.

about ice

A liquid becomes solid when it gets cold enough. Ice happens when water freezes. There can be ice anywhere there is water and the temperature is below freezing.

The ice crafts in this book are meant to be displayed outside when the temperature is below 32 degrees Fahrenheit. But you might find it easier to freeze a project indoors in the freezer. Just be sure to take it outside as soon as you remove it from the freezer. You don't want it to melt and make a mess!

If your ice craft won't come out of the **container** it was frozen in, dip the outside of the container in warm water until it loosens. Or let it sit in a warmer place for a few minutes.

WHat you'll need

Here are many of the things you will need to do the projects in this book. You can find some of them around the house or yard. You can get others at a craft store or hardware store.

faucet and water

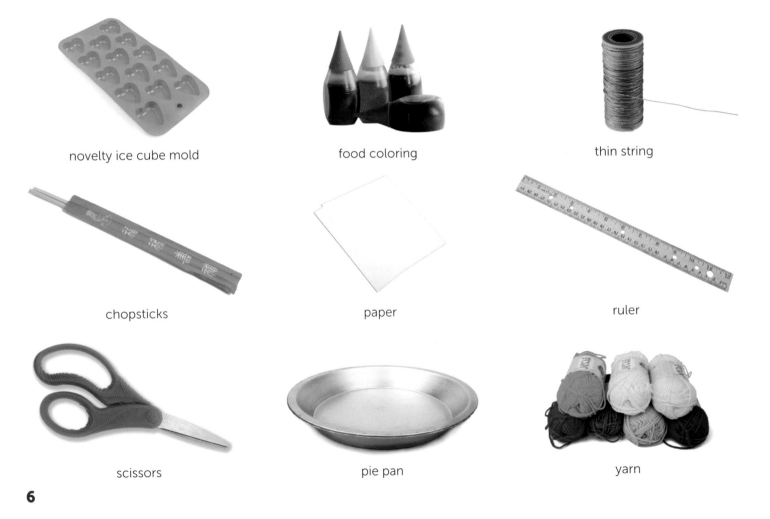

novelty ice cube mold

food coloring

thin string

chopsticks

paper

ruler

scissors

pie pan

yarn

balloons

cereal bowl

tea candles

foil pan

twigs and other natural materials

raffia

garden cutters

plastic bowls

small stones

ice cube tray

paper cups

small plastic container

ice cube garland

Festoon a fence with this groovy garland.

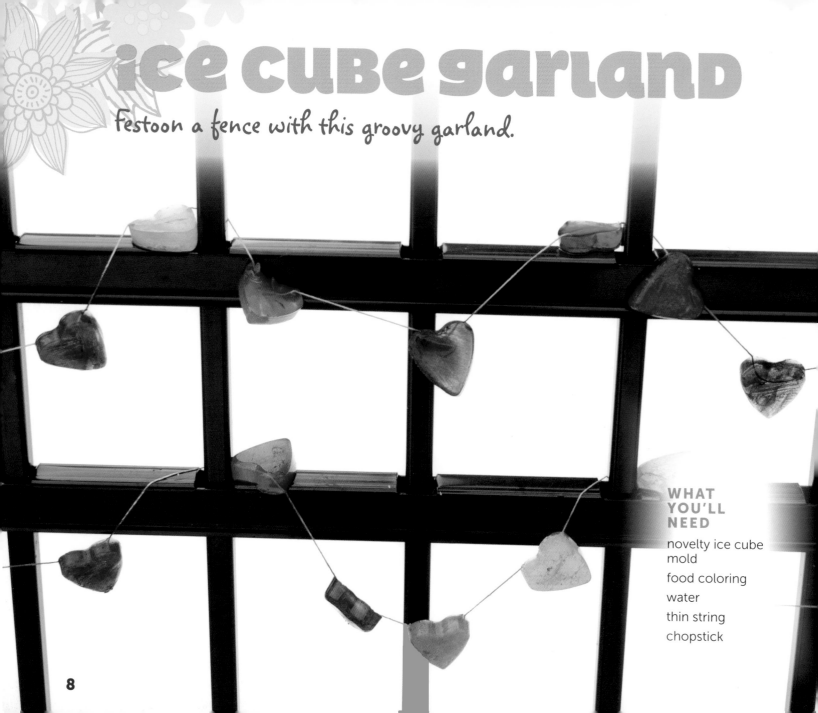

WHAT YOU'LL NEED

novelty ice cube mold

food coloring

water

thin string

chopstick

8

1 Put a few drops of food coloring in each ice cube space.

2 Fill each space with water.

3 Cut a long piece of string. Lay it over the tray.

4 Use a chopstick to poke the string down into each space.

5 Let the water freeze completely.

6 Pop the cubes out of the tray.

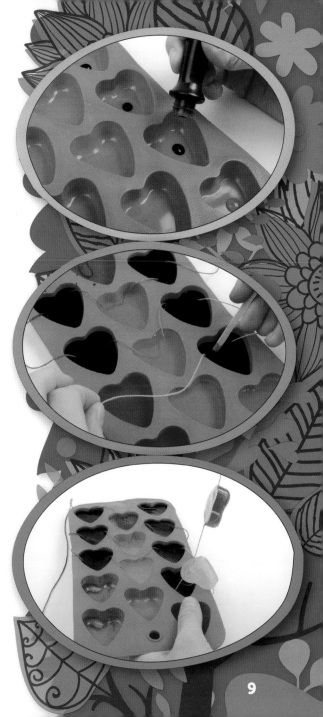

Pro tip
Wet the string before you use it. It will stay in the water better.

fun tip
You can use the colored cubes to make your drinks more fun. Just leave out the string when you freeze the tray.

snowflake Disk

Keep your eye on this icy dangler.

Paper Snowflake

1 Cut a 6-inch (15.2 cm) square of paper.

2 Fold the square in half to make a triangle.

3 Fold the triangle in half. Fold it in half again.

4 Hold the triangle by the longest edge. Cut the side of triangle with open edges. Round the cut so the snowflake will be round when you unfold it.

continued on the next page

5 Cut small pieces out of the two folded triangle sides. This will make the paper look like a snowflake.

6 Unfold the snowflake. Smooth it out.

FUN TIP

Your snowflake can be simple or fancy. Let your creativity go wild!

Disk

 Fill the pie tin with about 1 inch (2.5 cm) of water.

 Lay the paper snowflake in the water.

Press the snowflake into the water.

 Cut a 12-inch (30.5 cm) piece of yarn. Lay the ends in the water. The **loop** should hang over the side of the pan.

 Freeze the water.

 Pop the ice disk out of the pan.

🦋 variation

Make your disk a sun catcher. Put small pieces of different colors of paper in the water instead of a snowflake. When the sun shines through, the colors will glow!

COLORED BALLS

Add a blast of crazy color with these beautiful balls.

WHAT YOU'LL NEED

balloons
food coloring
faucet and water
scissors

1 Put a few drops of food coloring in a balloon.

2 Stretch the end of the balloon over the faucet. Hold the end around the faucet.

3 Turn on the water. Hold the balloon in your hand while it fills. Turn off the water.

continued on the next page

 get fancy

Use different sized balloons to make different sized balls.

 Pro tip

Use the freezer if there's no snow outside. Set each balloon in a bowl to make the bottoms round.

15

4 **Squeeze** the neck of the balloon closed. Pull it off the faucet. Tie the end of the balloon.

5 Repeat steps 1 through 4 for each ball you want to make.

6 Dig a hole in the snow for each balloon. Put the balloons in the holes. Pack snow around the balloons. The balloons will freeze in the shape of the holes.

7 Let the water freeze completely. Then remove the balloons from the snow.

8 Cut the top off each balloon. Peel the balloons off of the ice balls.

🐦 **fun fact**

Snow is a good **insulator**. It might take longer for the balloons to freeze in the snow than in the freezer!

HOLLOW LANTERN

Help light the way with a lovely lantern.

1 Stretch the end of a balloon over the faucet. Hold the end.

2 Turn on the water. Support the balloon in your hand while it fills. Make the balloon about the same size as the bowl. Turn off the water.

3 **Squeeze** the neck of the balloon closed. Pull it off the faucet. Tie the end of the balloon.

4 Put the balloon in the bowl. Put the bowl and balloon in the freezer.

5 Don't let the water freeze solid. Only let it freeze about halfway.

6 Take the balloon out of the bowl. Cut off the end of the balloon.

7 Break through the top of the ball. Pour out the water.

8 Peel the rest of the balloon away from the ice ball.

9 Place a tea light in the hollow ball.

 Pro tip

The water will freeze around the outside. After two hours, check the balloon every half hour. The ice should be thick enough that it doesn't break when you press on the side of the balloon. But it shouldn't be so thick that you can't break through the top.

letter squares

Spelling will be swell when you use an icy alphabet.

20

1 Form letters with the twigs and other **materials** you found. Tie the pieces together with raffia.

2 Arrange each letter in a pan.

3 Gently pour water into the pans. Reposition the letters if they move.

4 Let the water freeze completely.

5 Pop the letters out of the pans.

6 Arrange the letters to spell your word.

 Pro tip

The material you make the letter shapes with may float. Freeze each square in two steps. Fill the pan halfway and add the letter. Freeze it. Then add more water to cover the letter. Freeze it.

tea candle Holders

Tiny tea candles create a warm glow.

WHAT YOU'LL NEED

small plastic bowl

paper cups

small stones

tea candles

large plastic bowl

Single Candle Holder

 Fill the plastic bowl halfway with water.

2 Freeze the water completely.

3 Pour another 2 inches (5 cm) of water into the bowl.

4 Put a few small stones in a paper cup to weigh it down. Put it in the middle of the bowl.

5 Freeze the water completely.

continued on the next page

6 Take the stones out of the paper cup.

7 Fill the cup with warm water. Wait for the ice around the cup to melt. Remove the cup.

8 Remove the ice from the bowl.

9 Put a tea candle in the hole left by the paper cup.

 Pro tip

You can use anything to weigh down the paper cups. Rice, marbles, or coins work well too.

Multi Candle Holder

1   Use a large bowl. The larger the better!

2   Follow steps 1 through 3 from the Single Candle Holder (see page 23).

3   Put a few small stones in several paper cups to weigh them down.

4   Space the cups evenly around on the ice in the bowl.

5   Follow steps 5 through 8 from the Single Candle Holder (see pages 23 to 24).

6   Put a tea candle in each hole left by the paper cups.

rainbow wreath

You'll see the colors of the rainbow in this wreath.

WHAT YOU'LL NEED

ice cube tray
food coloring
water
pie pan
paper cup
small stones
raffia
scissors

26

1. Put a few drops of food coloring in each ice cube space. Fill each space with water. Freeze the ice cubes.

2. Fill the pie pan with water. Put a few small stones in a paper cup, Set it in the middle of the pan.

3. Freeze the water until there is a crust of ice on the top.

4. Break holes in the crust. Place the colored ice cubes in the icy water around the cup.

5. Freeze the water completely.

6. Remove the stones from the cup. Fill the cup with warm water. Wait for the ice around the cup to melt. Remove the cup.

7. Pop the ice wreath out of the pan. Tie raffia through the center hole to make a hanger.

fun tip

Use the Rainbow Wreath as a holiday helper! Keep your drinks cool by putting the wreath in a bowl filled with fruit punch.

Pom-pom ornaments

Pom-pom ice ornaments will pep up the place!

WHAT YOU'LL NEED

yarn

ruler

scissors

small plastic container

water

28

Pom-pom

1 Wrap yarn around your fingers to make a **bundle**.

2 Slip the yarn off your fingers. Keep the **loops** together.

3 Wrap a 12-inch (30.5 cm) piece of yarn around the middle of the bundle. Pull it tight. Tie a knot. Tie the ends together to make a hanger.

4 Cut the loops on each side of the bundle.

5 **Fluff** the pom-pom. Trim any uneven ends.

continued on the next page

Ornament

1 Put the pom-pom in the plastic **container**. Lay the hanger over the side of the container.

2 Fill the container with enough water to cover the pom-pom.

3 **Squeeze** the pom-pom to **soak** the yarn. This keeps the pom-pom from floating.

4 Freeze the water completely.

5 Use the hanger to pull the pom-pom ornament out of the container.

conclusion

Isn't ice great? You have let the beauty of nature come through with these wonderful ice crafts. If you had fun, don't stop here. How else can you use ice?

And check out the other books in the Super Simple Nature Crafts series. You'll find projects that use leaves, pinecones, pressed flowers, seashells, and twigs. The ideas are endless!

glossary

bundle – a group of things tied together.

Celsius – a scale used to measure temperature in the metric system.

container – something that other things can be put into.

degree – the unit used to measure temperature.

fluff – to loosen or separate.

icicle – a hanging point of ice formed when dripping water freezes.

insulator – something that keeps heat or cold in or out.

loop – a circle made by a rope, string, or thread.

material – something that other things can be made of, such as fabric, wood, or metal.

soak – to make completely wet.

squeeze – to press the sides of something together.